EXPLORING WORLD CULTURES

Saudi Arabia

Laura L. Sullivan

Cavendish
Square

New York

Library of Congress Cataloging-in-Publication Data

Names: Sullivan, Laura L., 1974- author.
Title: Saudi Arabia / Laura L. Sullivan.
Other titles: Exploring world cultures.
Description: New York : Cavendish Square Publishing, 2018. | Series: Exploring world cultures | Includes index.
Identifiers: LCCN 2016049400 (print) | LCCN 2016057525 (ebook) | ISBN 9781502624918 (pbk.) | ISBN 9781502624888 (6 pack) | ISBN 9781502624901 (library bound) | ISBN 9781502624895 (E-book)
Subjects: LCSH: Saudi Arabia--Juvenile literature.
Classification: LCC DS204.25 .S85 2018 (print) | LCC DS204.25 (ebook) | DDC 953.8--dc23
LC record available at HYPERLINK "https://lccn.loc.gov/2016049400" https://lccn.loc.gov/2016049400

Editorial Director: David McNamara
Editor: Kristen Susienka
Copy Editor: Rebecca Rohan
Associate Art Director: Amy Greenan
Designer: Joseph Macri
Production Coordinator: Karol Szymczuk
Photo Research: J8 Media

Contents

Saudi Arabia is a land of tradition and modernity.

The Kingdom of Saudi Arabia is a desert country located on the Arabian Peninsula. It is a rich country with a lot of oil. It is a **conservative** society, where women have few rights.

Many people there follow a religion called Islam. Mecca and Medina, two of Islam's holy sites, are in Saudi Arabia.

Saudi Arabia is usually considered an **ally** of the United States. However, there have been some difficulties since the September 11, 2001, terrorist attacks because most of the attackers were from Saudi Arabia.

The country has many unique traditions and customs. Come learn more about Saudi Arabia.

Saudi Arabia lies on the Arabian Peninsula. It is a large country, about 830,000 square miles (2,149,690 square kilometers). Nearly all of the country is desert. There are almost no lakes or rivers. The country does have many **wadis**. These dry riverbeds fill with water at different times during the year. These are some of the

A map of Saudi Arabia and its neighbors

FACT!

Saudi Arabia is about one-third the size of the continental United States.

places crops can be grown. Saudi Arabia has coastlines on the Persian Gulf and the Red Sea. To the north are the countries of Iraq, Jordan, and Kuwait. To the south and east are Yemen, Oman, the United Arab Emirates, Bahrain, and Qatar.

Some Saudi cities have skyscrapers. Others have more traditional buildings.

Weather and Climate

In general, Saudi Arabian days are hot, but nights can be frosty. Monsoons, or heavy storms, blow through in winter and spring. The area gets 12 to 20 inches (30 to 50 centimeters) of rain a year.

History

Before the seventh century CE, many separate **nomadic** tribes lived in Saudi Arabia. The Prophet Muhammad was born around 571 CE. He founded the Islamic religion. He brought the tribes together, and after his death, the people

King Abdulaziz ibn Saud founded Saudi Arabia.

who ruled came to control much of the Middle East and beyond. Their power stretched as far as Spain and Pakistan. Later, the Islamic government moved to other areas, and Saudi Arabia was again mostly run by tribes.

The First King

Abdulaziz ibn Saud founded Saudi Arabia in 1932 and was its first king. He had forty-five sons. All kings of Saudi Arabia are his descendants.

The area remained important because of Mecca and Medina. The region officially became the Kingdom of Saudi Arabia in 1932. It wasn't until the discovery of oil in 1938 that Saudi Arabia became a world power.

Saudi Arabia is known for its oil.

FACT!

Humans have lived in the area now known as Saudi Arabia for about twenty thousand years.

Government

The king of Saudi Arabia is the head of the government. He makes **decrees**. He must follow sharia, or Islamic religious law. Members of the royal family hold most other high government positions. There are no national

King Salman bin Abdulaziz al-Saud, seen here with US president Barack Obama

elections and no political parties. People can vote in local elections, though.

All adult males have the right to present a petition (or formal request) directly to the king.

Votes for Women

Women in Saudi Arabia weren't allowed to vote until 2015. Then, they could vote for local candidates and run for local office.

One group that holds power in Saudi Arabia is the *ulama*. This group of religious judges and leaders makes many decisions. They work together with the king. The **Quran** and the teachings of the Prophet Muhammad form the

Saudi women were first allowed to vote in 2015.

country's constitution, or document of laws. The current king is King Salman bin Abdulaziz al-Saud. He lives in the capital, Riyadh.

The Economy

Most of Saudi Arabia's **economy** relies on oil. Today, the country holds 18 percent of the world's oil reserves. Many people working in the oil industry come from countries outside of Saudi Arabia.

Dates, which grow on palms, are among the most widely grown foods in Saudi Arabia.

FACT!

Besides oil, Saudi Arabia has other natural resources, including copper, zinc, silver, gold, phosphate, and tungsten.

A Trip to Mecca

Every year, more than two million Muslims travel to the holy city of Mecca on a hajj, or religious pilgrimage. The hajj can add $3 billion to the economy.

The hajj helps boost the country's economy.

The economy also depends on construction work and real estate sales. Despite the dry desert climate, some farming happens. Crops need water to survive. It is not easy to get. Special water called desalinated water costs a lot of money. There is water underground, but it is being used up quickly. A crop that grows well without lots of water is dates. They are widely grown in Saudi Arabia.

The Environment

Saudi Arabia has many animals and plants. Large mammals include hyenas, baboons, and Arabian wolves. Reptiles such as snakes and lizards thrive in the desert. Many birds of prey soar in the skies.

The Arabian oryx was once extinct in the wild, but is making a comeback.

Unicorns?

The Arabian oryx might have inspired the unicorn myth. It went extinct in the wild in the 1970s. Some remained in captivity and eventually were returned to the wild. Today, there are over one thousand in Saudi Arabia.

The country faces environmental problems. For one, there is not a lot of water there. Most water is pumped from the ground and used up. Another problem is pollution. Chemicals from

Camels are pets in Saudi Arabia, not wild.

cars and trucks make the air dirty.

Oil can also harm the environment. Oil spills have damaged the coastlines and killed animals that live nearby.

FACT!

One of Saudi Arabia's laws says: "The State shall endeavor to preserve, protect, and improve the environment, and prevent pollution."

Almost twenty-seven million people live in Saudi Arabia. Of those, as many as ten million are immigrants. Most of these people are in the country to work. They come from India, Pakistan, the Philippines, and Indonesia. About 90 percent of the people living in Saudi Arabia are Arabs.

Two women sort through clothing at a market.

About one hundred thousand Westerners (from Europe or North America) live in Saudi Arabia.

The country is known for having a very religious, conservative culture. Though historically most of the people who lived in Saudi Arabia were nomadic, today most people live in cities. The three largest cities are Riyadh, Jeddah, and Mecca. The population is very young. About 60 percent of the population is under twenty-one years old.

Citizenship

Non-Muslims aren't allowed to live permanently in the country. Muslims from other countries who have lived in Saudi Arabia for ten years are allowed to apply to become citizens.

Life in Saudi Arabia tends to be very traditional. Many customs are passed down through generations. Saudi Arabians are conservative and religious. Families are often large.

Women have limited rights. They

Women, such as these journalists, have to cover most of their bodies in public.

aren't allowed to drive and were only recently allowed to vote. Every woman has to have a male guardian when in public. However, most Saudi Arabian women are well educated, and many work outside of the home. Inside the family, women often have great power.

Clothes

Men usually wear a *thawb*, or long robe with long sleeves. In summer it is white, and in cooler weather it might be in darker colors. All women have to wear a long black robe called an *abaya* when they are in public. They usually cover their hair and wear a veil.

FACT!

Men often greet both friends and strangers with embraces but are forbidden from touching women they aren't related to.

Saudi men greet each other with an embrace.

19

Religion

The official religion of Saudi Arabia is Islam. It states that there is one god, Allah, and Muhammad is his prophet. The holy book is the Quran. Muslims (those who practice Islam) follow the Five Pillars of Islam: faith, prayer, charity, fasting, and pilgrimage.

Muslims are expected to pray five times a day.

There are non-Muslims, like Hindus, Buddhists, or Christians, living there too. They are not allowed to practice their religion. Atheists (people who don't believe in any god) are considered terrorists.

Hajj

Every Muslim is expected to make a pilgrimage, or religious journey, to Mecca once in their lifetime. Mecca is where the Prophet Muhammad was born. It is the holiest city in the Islamic world.

Pilgrims touch the Black Stone at Mecca.

FACT!

During the month of Ramadan, almost all Muslims fast from eating for certain periods. They do not eat or drink anything from sunrise to sunset. After dark and before dawn, they can eat and drink again.

Language

Arabic is the official language of Saudi Arabia. Classical Arabic is the language of the Quran. In Saudi Arabia, there are three **dialects** of Arabic. Sometimes the dialects sound so different that it is hard for people to understand each other, even though they are all speaking Arabic.

This script reads, "There is no god but God. Muhammad is the messenger of God."

FACT!

Written Arabic is an *abjad* language. That is, the letters represent consonants. Most of the time, vowels aren't indicated or are shown by extra marks.

The Arabic language is written with the Arabic alphabet. The script is written and read from right to left. Arabic calligraphy is used as decoration, an art form, and for religious purposes.

Arabic Words

The English language has several words with Arabic origins. Many of those words begin with "al," such as alcohol, algebra, and albatross. Other words include candy, coffee, jar, magazine, and zero.

Arts and Festivals

Saudi Arabians enjoy music, dance, and visual arts. Islam forbids showing the human form in artwork, so much of Islamic art is calligraphy, floral designs, or geometric patterns. Music is usually based on poetry. Men sometimes perform a warlike dance involving swords.

Saudi men do a sword dance called *al ardah*.

In 1980, all theaters and cinemas were shut down. Today, the only movie theater is an IMAX in the city of Khobar. Most Saudi Arabians watch movies and shows from around the world in their homes.

24

Authors

Because of laws in the country, authors struggle to express themselves freely. Novelists popular in other countries may be persecuted at home.

Writer Raif Badawi was punished for his works.

Jenadriya is a two-week festival of Saudi Arabian culture. It takes place in January or February. The festival features horse and camel racing, poetry recitals, and traditional arts and crafts like woodworking, pottery, and weaving.

Poetry by the Bedouin, traditional nomadic tribes, is one of the most popular art forms in Saudi Arabia.

Soccer (called football in Saudi Arabia) is the most popular sport in Saudi Arabia. The national team has played in the Asian Cup and the World Cup several times. Basketball is also widely attended.

Wojdan Shaherkani competes in the Olympics.

In the hot weather, people enjoy water sports and activities. Sailing, swimming, and scuba diving are fun activities to do.

FACT!

Camel racing has used very young, small children as jockeys (riders). Today, some tracks use robots with whips instead.

Some sports are unique to Saudi Arabia and a few neighboring countries. People attend camel races. These desert animals can sprint at 40 miles per hour (64 kilometers per hour), or run at 25 miles per hour (40 kmh) for an hour or more. Falconry is another favorite traditional activity.

Women in Sports

Women generally don't participate in sports in school. If they do, they have to train and play completely separate from men. The first two Saudi Arabian women competed in the Olympic Games in 2012, in running and judo.

Food

Saudi Arabian food must follow Islamic laws about diet. All pig products are forbidden. So is alcohol. Any animal used for food must be killed and prepared in a *halal* way. That means the animal must be prayed over in the name of Allah before it is killed.

Saudis serve coffee to show hospitality to guests.

Lamb is one of the most popular foods. **Kebabs** are widely eaten. Flatbread and dates are served at most meals.

It is considered good manners to eat a lot and burp to show appreciation of the food.

Coffee is served as part of a ceremony of hospitality. Other common drinks include tea, sheep's milk, goat's milk, camel milk, and laban (a **fermented** milk served either sweet or salty).

Kebabs are popular meals in Saudi Arabia.

Finger Food

Food is often eaten with the fingers or by using a piece of bread as a scoop. In Saudi Arabia, only the right hand should be used to touch food.

Glossary

ally
A country that agrees to cooperate with another country.

conservative
Having traditional attitudes about religion or politics.

decree
An official announcement.

dialect
A version of a language.

economy
The activities of a country that bring the country money.

fermented
Rotting or decomposed.

kebab
A meal of meat or vegetables placed on a stick.

nomadic
Traveling from place to place rather than having a permanent home.

Quran
The holy book of Islam.

wadi
A valley or channel that is usually dry except in the rainy season.

Find Out More

Books

1001 Inventions and Awesome Facts from Muslim Civilization. Washington, DC: National Geographic Children's Books, 2012.

Stone, Caroline. *DK Eyewitness Books: Islam*. New York: DK Children, 2005.

Website

Ducksters: Saudi Arabia

http://www.ducksters.com/geography/country.php?country=Saudi%20Arabia

Video

Saudi Arabia: Culture and Heritage

https://www.youtube.com/watch?v=fWw2QZ7zbeQ

A video collage shows scenes from Saudi Arabia

Index

About the Author

Laura L. Sullivan is the author of more than thirty fiction and nonfiction books for children, including the fantasies *Under the Green Hill* and *Guardian of the Green Hill*. She has written many books for Cavendish Square.